VIA Folios 181

The Widowing Radiance

Published by Bordighera Press, an imprint of the John D. Calandra Italian American Institute of Queens College, The City University of New York.

25 West 43rd Street, 17th Floor, New York, NY 10036

Library of Congress Control Number: 2025931716

Cover image by Charity Kittler.

VIA Folios 181
ISBN 978-1-59954-231-7

THE
WIDOWING
RADIANCE

DANTE DI STEFANO

BORDIGHERA PRESS

for Mom
for my brother, Daeman
for Harvey (H.L. Hix)

Table of Contents

No doubt there's truth to Frost's famous formulation that poetry offers "a momentary stay against confusion," but I'm more intent, as a writer of poetry and as a reader of poetry, on tapping into another capacity of poetry, its ability to offer — to *be* — a provisional stay against reduction.

H.L. HIX

Yonder, yes yonder, yonder, / yonder.

GERARD MANLEY HOPKINS

Prologue (Leaflet: To Marie Howe Here on Earth and to Jason Shinder in the Crystalline Sphere of Dante's *Paradiso*, Canto XXVII)

Sometimes everything is clear.
      The poem unlooses it-
self from armpit & eyeball
          & knotted muscle & groin
     & arthritic joint & gut.

The poem ascends into
     a daydream of first kisses
& fourth grade & all the slips
         & missteps that ladder up
    a life beginning at birth,

or perhaps at death & re-
     wound backwards to form the frame
of a consciousness flaring
        into being for one brief
    barely audible wingbeat.

In a story, time takes no
     time, an old Sicilian
proverb says, but also, I
        think, in the beam-bearing years
    of an existence, time takes

the same way. The simple song
       of the angels is always
pouring into us, even those
           of us who don't believe in
      such strange sky-blue presences.

Marie, we live in a time of
       postscripts & chainsaws, a time
to die & die & die in,
           till you die. Your Persephone
      scrambles atop Kunitz's

testing-tree & croons a dark
       refrain, the handful of truths
poetry can hold—I will
           dance on my shadow. If there
      is no cure, I still want to

correct a few things. Let me,
       let me keep on describing
things to be sure they happened.
           Let me sing the stupid hope,
     ringing, ringing in my throat—

i. (Rain Inscription)

Let's begin with the way rain
          lovingly inscribes itself
into the loam of one of
                  those square states out west. There you
          are, writing letters throughout

the night, addressing yourself
          to the ghosts & the blackbirds
alighting on your eyebrows
               & carotid arteries,
          prophesying five more months

of deep & endless winter
          while the world divests itself
of paradox & begins
               another twenty-four hour
          news cycle no one watches.

Poor world, poor world, O poor, poor
          world, I say to the likeness
of my father's face looking
               back at me in the mirror.
          Life is one long unresolved

string of correspondences,
            wouldn't you agree? Nothing
attested, everything sung.
                    Or as you say Oppen says,
            "Each of us knows only one

thing for himself, & says that
            in the poems." I prefer
the shovel's shrug as it breaks
                    hard earth & the ecstatic
            irritant of dirt under

my nails signaling the blooms
            to come after the burning
bush has been planted and doused
                    with the kerosene phoneme
            of a single simple sigh.

That's not true, though. I'm not
            a gardener. Why did I
feel the need to pretend to
                    be one? To satisfy some
            odd inkling toward lyric?

Still, God bless the stillness gapped
            between us as easy as
lying—glass swept up into
                    the dust pile & then sparkling
            unseen among the coffee

grounds & arugula in
            the tall lavender-scented
Glad garbage bag, discreetly
                    hidden away under new
            polished marble countertops

in a recently redone
       kitchen in suburbs somewhere
between Wyoming & up-
          state New York. Harvey, outside
     right now, a male cardinal

swoops toward the window that
       frames the backyard as I write,
& just before he hits the pane
          he banks like a flying saucer,
     leaving me with a bright red

brush stroke on the memory
       of another moment—spare,
counter, original, & strange—
          I can neither be done with
     nor be sure of, like all poems.

ii. (As Easy As Lying)

A poet's preparation
      begins outside the poem's
windowpanes. It begins
         in sparrow & fern & red
    wagon pulled by a father.

The father may be a good
      father or a bad father.
He may hold the sparrow in
         his hand or he may berate
    the redness of the wagon.

It passes through the curveballs
      swung at & missed in hundreds
of nighttime little league games.
         It ends in the glyphs of heart
    monitors flatlined right here.

& maybe the sparrows are
      really juncos or blue jays.
& maybe the fern wasn't
         really there. Maybe it was
    a marigold I planted

because I was getting sad
        & sentimental, thinking
of my grandmother's garden
            full of marigolds, lilies,
        & flagrant lilac bushes.

Harvey, I'm writing you this
        self-portrait of a poem,
this poem as self-portrait
            in the manner of your work,
        by which I mean in the grain

of the grains of sand draining
        from an antique hourglass held
in the hands of a Mayan
            astronomer, come unstuck
        in time as it unfolds as

poetry. Is it true we
        spend our lives trying to re-
member the future & fail-
            ing to form the right questions?
        What makes heaven legible?

Why did I love ferns so much
        as a kid? Why did being
together on holidays
            always make me feel lonely?
        Why does the vague ache of that

remembered feeling throb like
        every poem I've ever
dwelt in? Why can I feel those
            words flying in my knuckles
        as I write this dialogue

for one? Why do I feel home-
　　　　sick & heady all at once?
Why is autumn in New York
　　　　　　always sweeping into me?
　　　　Why is my voice cracking like

a middle school chorister?
　　　　Why am I always looking for
the song under the song that
　　　　　　the river of bees sings to
　　　　the snakeskin shed in the hive?

Is that last one a nonsense
　　　　question? Is a perfect hell
made of sound without silence?
　　　　　　Why do human beings think
　　　　they're better than grass, air, stone?

iii. (Legible Heavens)

To imagine my life made
        legible to others, first
I imagine your life laid
                out in the star charts augured
        in the innards of the wren,

in the tornado's funnel
        twisting through the lines of this
poem, in the jade beads draped
                upon the beloved's chest,
        in the infinite yellow

of old photographs, a room
        where a marionette hung
in the corner, terrific
                as a crucifix transformed
        into a swift grim biplane

passing through the edges of
        a Chagall painting I dream
myself into each evening.
                I see your life a burning
        dream, a shrill declension of

wingbeats, a body broken
        into a murder of crows,
buttercups lamenting bird-
                laden maples, a hundred
        hundred summers lived at once.

"Gods ignite themselves like snow,"
        you wrote, to get at something
beyond simple saying: fire
                of cock and clitoris, throb
        and thrum and gush and whisper,

the braille of downy arm hair.
        I gather beatitudes
and sing along with them as
                if they were a playlist:
        Replete, are the breathless; theirs

are the skies. Replete, those who
        grieve, who must be consoled…who
stake no claim, those who give to
                others mercy. Replete, all
        who suffer for doing good.

Harvey, I continue to
        solicit, like you, miracles
I mustn't expect: grace from
                the black that bookends a life—
        to hold my children, my spouse,

the dog asleep on the couch
        as I write this, forever,
in this unfolding moment,
                repeating and repeating
        this particular Eden

while in one of your earliest
        poems you remark that some
things are worth a life, by which
            I think you mean, a lifetime,
        like light rain, a woman's back

asleep beside you as you
        compose and decompose poems,
the long leaves of bamboo shoots,
            rubbing jointly in the dark,
        become lines of inquiry.

iv. (Interleaf: To My Dead Father)

You always appear before
        me as you did on your death-
bed, an hour before you went
            mute one last time, when you could
        still garble together some

scraps of phrases & when you
        asked me to scratch your back, those
silver and black hairs, filaments
            attached to the underworld,
        & no feeling in me then,

except patience & calm like
        the center of a poem
when I'm writing it, like this
            moment right now when I'm
        calling out to nothingness,

to the eye of nothingness
        you now occupy as I will
at some point. I keep pouring
            you into poems & still
        I never say what I need

said, as if I could ever
        do so, in poem or in
person; something's always caught
            in the throat & ribbiting
        outward. I usually feel

angry at you & say so,
        but as my grudges accrue,
they add up to less & less.
            A parent is always a
        stranger, a vault, a tomb with

the stone rolled away, a grave
        grown empty in the fullness
of time, the rumor of some kind
            of rising, a myth fleshed
        the way words seem to ascend,

only words don't really save
        or ascend. Instead, they trend
toward dawdle & dandle
            & sprawl & rivering out
        into a diamonded sea.

The point is, dad, despite it
        all, I am always holding
your body as I carry
            you almost to your hospice
        bed & your last breath becomes

this same poem that I keep
        rewriting just below my
ribcage & composed of flit
            & ache & be & bee &
        Emily Dickinson's scrawled

lines, domains enveloping,
        I & you & all the rest
of everybody in the
                pocket of the dress of this
    universe you've blinked out of.

v. (Lines of Inquiry)

My wife is putting to bed
        our daughter. My son sleeps in
his crib. The dog curls himself
            into a question mark on
      the couch. I'm in the basement

once again, weaving through *Lines*
        of Inquiry. The winter
syntax of the new year comes
            rapping at the windowpane
      behind the Venetian blinds

in front of me. I'm thinking
        about the line: "…my very
living measures my distance
            from the good, I understood
      from *Antigone*," & then

I'm thinking of the baby
        mouse I caught in the humane
trap this morning & how I
            let it loose in the street in
      front of my house & watched it

zigzag across the asphalt
        to the neighbor's lawn, whose cat
watched too from her living room.
            & I'm thinking of my son
    falling asleep in my lap,

holding my index finger,
        holding the winter syntax
of safety and snugness in
            his bones, holding the syntax
    of sweetness by its long scarf

whipping in the December
        wind, this sweet son whose bones I
bow to—I think of him &
            all the lines I'm trying to
    follow unravel. & all

I want is to understand
        something about enduring
the way the three flames suffer
            to blaze from the cinnamon
    apple Glade candle behind

me on the bookcase. Heaven
        is in the storebought slightly
antiseptic scent. Heaven
            is in the treatise disguised
    as a sonnet's last couplet.

Heaven is in the tiny
        fingers clasping my finger
at bedtime. Heaven is when
            our five-year-old daughter climbs
    into our bed & we're too

tired to carry her back to
        her own room. Heaven is a
a dining room with crayoned
            walls & crumbs on the counters
      & too little sleep & no

time for poems, but poems
        nonetheless, poems written
with backwards e's in pastel
          & red stick figure angels
        hovering above each threshold.

Who cares about the good? Or
        one's distance from it? I'll take
my Crayola Picasso,
           the chiaroscuro of
      the mice lost in cabinets

& wandering heating ducts
        throughout the suburbs of this
poem I keep finding myself
          immersed in, this poem whose
      audience is one: you, me,

the two of us, reader &
        writer, poet & poet,
& poem leafing to life
          in some imagined April
      held in the vase of our hands.

vi. (Perfect Hell)

God bless the plump blackberries
           & rotting fenceposts ebbing
in memory, receding
               into the undergrowth of
my misfiring frontal lobe.

I find myself more and more
           like that line of yours, Harvey:
"like a dove's breast sliced in two
              by a boy's knife." I open
my wounds to a seam of wind.

I am the boy & the dove
           & the knife & the wound &
the wind that catches the sail
             of a stanza & pulls taut
the canvas of unsaying.

My five-year-old daughter said:
           "keep it attracted in your
mouth" when I was about to
             say something she didn't want
said & again I was charmed

by the strange poetry of
        children, which is much wilder
than anything I can comb
            from diaphragm to margin
        to cerebellum & back.

Dante made hell perfect &
        the provenance of middle
age. It's easy to forget
            the inverted calendars
        that hold a life in place,

the fact that the silhouette
        of a leaf & branch is not
shot through with divine chlorophyll,
            that home is a small doorway
        the kayaking butterfly

of the heart keeps paddling-
        cartwheeling-lighting out from.
Remember, to hold each up-
            side down day of the week close:
        daytime hours—paper diamonds

scissored to life so gently.
        That want & want is a dream
house, that later is right now
            unfolding-falling-snipping
        full circles in the endless

air. Remember, the little
        beings afoot in the half-
moon of your home keep calling
            you to a fullness beyond
        mere unsaying & silence

like when your five-year-old said
          on a blustery thirteenth
of the month, "let's go outside
              & adore the wind." Like here:
          inside this section's last line.

vii. (American Anger)

Life is a long widowing
          radiance. You walk the one
winding staircase encoded
                    in your own DNA strands
          & find there your beloved

dead & dying rising as
          if ascending a shining
escalator to heaven
                    in an unscripted sitcom
          where the recurring theme is

a laugh-tracked belligerence.
          Harvey, you wrote: "keep the cheap
piano, but give me back
                    my yellowed stack of unplayed
          sheet music, my criminal

love." Or "kleptomaniac
          love" instead of "criminal."
I forget which, but your words
                    keep coiling into me like
          the snake in the Gadsden flag.

What you're always insisting
         on is the way the word makes
flesh & is made flesh & dwells
              among us, even at
         last gasp, at grasp, & grapple.

We live under the sway of
         screen after screen, none of them
framed & hinged on a threshold,
              each aperture a rupture,
         a wound exposing sinew

& the viscera below.
         In my earbuds, harpsicords
sprout adagio in G
              minor in a Sonata
         by Albinoni or is

it solo piano in
         a dream of Thelonious
Monk's "Misterioso" live
              at the Five Spot, explaining
         America to me in

the mode of an off-kilter
         abecedarian: A
is for Arapaho, apt
              antonym for Anglican
         oppression. B is for blues

as in Big Bill Broonzy, B.
         B. King, & Billie H.
singing "Autumn in New York"
              forever on repeat in
         the livestream of my heartbeat.

C is for concrete, Chrysler,
        Coca-Cola in a Frank
O'Hara poem, spilling
           all over the confession:
      "All I want is boundless love."

D is for Destiny, as
        in "Manifest," Detroit as
in "Red" in a Spike Lee joint,
          as in Democracy
      spinning like a loose hubcap.

E is for extinct eagle,
        is for exempt & extort
& egalitarian
           éclat endlessly ebbing
      in edits. Exeunt Omnis.

F is for French fries, as in
        fast food, as in the golden
arches filleting all your
           finest filigreed daydreams
      of freedom from farce & fear.

G is for greed, goddammit,
        of course, & Ginsberg dressed as
Uncle Sam at Golgotha,
           inscribing grim gray matter
      gnostic psalms on *Leaves of Grass.*

H is for Halt, as in here,
        hover over the cursor
for a half-millisecond
          & resolve this alphabet
      in someone else's heaven.

The heaven of the double
      H alliterated in
your name, Harvey Hix, heaving
          against hagiography,
     the unsainting instant of this

poem meandering toward
      the hyperbole of its
afterlife on page & in
          the wind unwinding my lungs,
     galloping out & out &—

viii. (Interleaf: To My Living Mother)

You loom. Frame, apparatus,
      for interlacing the threads
of sense & memory &
          self. You loom. Into sight. Take
      shape like mist or water or

the reflection of the moon
        on running water, on
braids of stream. I see your brown
          hair enwreathing me as you
      bend to the crib to free me.

From swaddle. First warmth. First milk.
      First bower. First port. Portal
through which my nostrils took in
         the wild yarns of oxygen.
      Why is it so hard to write

about you? To you? Past you?
      Mom, I see you as you are
now, your thinning gray hair lain
        across your granddaughter's wrist,
      my child a tributary

of you, of my wife's mother
        dead from Glioblastoma,
your husband dead from cancers
            of the pancreas and throat,
      the retinue of your dead

multiplying in the dark,
        the expanding universe
of grief an inhalation,
          an exhalation breaking
      into song after song &

aftersong. What's *aftersong*?
        It's the what of you I'll take
with me always from nightlight
          to last light of final breath.
      The *aftersong* of my wife

the only real legacy
        we will bequeath our children.
My wife's brown hair lain over
          your wrist, this daughtering light
      winging through your widowhood.

& winging too the anger,
        the pain, the grief of too much
bad architecture of the
          unsaid, locked in the basement,
      sitting on the weight bench, cowed

by the dark even in the light
        of afternoon filtering
in through the horizontal
          windows of decades, eons,
      of *aftersong* afterthought.

All I can say to you, mom,
      is this *aftersong*, is this
ineffable strand: sunlight
         on ripples over rocks, down
      mountainside to endless green.

ix. (First Fire, Then Birds)

I coast in someone else's
        heaven—inside a poem
I did not write—summoning:
           "God's two wills, *Screen Door Banging*
      in the Wind and *Melting Snow*

Sliding off a Windsheild…" Then,
        I repeat the refrain: "I
love the world, as any dancer,
            with the tips of my toes." I
      write to keep my body strung

through the eye of a camel—
        to keep my body kestrel-
hovering in the haint blue.
           I write to ward, off toward,
      to invoke congregations

of ghosts to sing through my throat.
        I'm writing right now to reach
something in myself that is
           in you, the you whom is I
      & whom isn't, who's sitting

astride the ampersand of:
        of my mind & holding forth—
Harvey Hix, poet, unnamed
                reader, friend, family, son,
        daughter, wife, mother, brother,

impossible coworker,
        student of melancholy
& ark of jubilation,
                arch interlocutor of
        this endless instant called *home*

I home toward in the line,
        in the line break, in the room
inside the room the stanza makes
                on the page & in the air
        where I've nested my desires.

I am flying away &
        toward the future in which I
have dissolved into typo
                & typography. I see
        my children there, running their

arthritic old forefingers
        across this very draft of
sunlight, across this motion,
                my jagged consciousness flared
        & flayed in Garamond font.

It's strange to dream my young ones
        old, but comforting to think
they might carry a part of
                me on leaf after leaf to
        leaf through once I've gone, to leaf

to life the one who writes these
        words as rain falls heavy on
the streets outside & I look
           on leafless tree & raindrop
      & songless stone alike with

love (my son, my daughter), read
        the fronds of my heart, leaflets
of my phonemes broken on
           the crosscurrents of brain &
      birdsong. All I want is to end

in song, the midwhistle in
        the will of a god, god of
screen doors slamming & endless
           want & wind in a box &
      snow sliding off the windshield.

x. (Chromatic)

A Love Supreme says: "Truth is
        I am nothing. Truth is too
I could not make myself so,
              or see myself so by my-
      self. I needed *it*, my no-

thingness. Now I hear." & Trane
        shaclacks into cattle car
& *Shoah Train* & cinder
           in the smokestack become Star
      of David, of Bethlehem,

the black milk of daybreak, of
        atom bomb & E =,
of black codes & black ops &
           blackwater & the montage
      from Spike Lee's *Bamboozled* &

Stevie Wonder singing "In
        1492, you came
upon these shores…" of the whole
           untold history of whip,
      chain, handcuff, baton, taser,

mace, zip-tie, suspension of
        Habeas Corpus, of Trane
wailing back from ziggurat to
              the moon landing, from embalmed
        pharaoh, alien probe making

first contact—all brutality
        in history jettisoned—
a golden record hurtling
            through the interstellar
        dark. All we have as humans

is atrocity & song.
        In America, trauma
& rage dovetail, counterclaim
            us, ask us to author an
        empire from epidermis

meeting bark. It is a strange
        time we live in like any
other & I for one can
            only fathom the world as
        c(h)ord, umbilicus of

the god of interleaf &
        aftersong & underdog
& one note repeated as
            one note as one note as one
        note as one note called leaflet

called love called home called song called
        loom & coast & wren & throat
& caw & poet & cluck
           & flock & bed & blackbird
        & wildflower-strewn garden.

xi. (Counterclaims)

Poems reawaken us
    to the pleasure of the un-
intelligibility
        of the world, Longenbach said.
    Poem as echo, echo-

location of self-amidst-
        the-ruin-the-weltering-
amidst. Poems as untalk,
            as unchained pit bull raging
    through the neighborhood, picking

up chihuahuas by the neck
        & shaking them in the street.
Poem as incisor-pierced
            scruff of the—poem as spin-
    drift & wilding orchard edge.

Poetry makes ever real
        to me my unreality.
My unreality clucks
            its tongue at me & pairs me
    with whomever reads these words.

We become conjoined twins as
        you continue through this long
poem with all its motley
                wrongness. Poem as unright.
        Poem as rite of wrongness.

Poem as sinew, as crack
        in the sidewalk you never
circumambulate. "Asking
                what poetry *does* misses
        what poetry *is*. & vice

versa." Poetry as field,
        as farrow, as plow, as fold.
Poetry as uncoupling
                of binaries. Poetry:
        against & against *against*.

Poetry holds the family
        pet's head in its hands & lifts
his muzzle up to inspect
                eternity in his eyes;
        god is the good dog's pupil.

& I am dilating out
        into another senseless
meaning beyond sense, the pitched
                space between the atmosphere
        & the satellite circling.

xii. (Interleaf: To Rachel Zucker)

At an AWP offsite
        reading, I was reading part
of the first long poem I wrote
            & after I read, the next
        poet who read mentioned that

the trailer for the new John
        Wick movie was running on
the TV screens behind me
            in the bar, & so he thought
        of my poem as fused now

to Keanu Reeves shooting up
        cathedrals & jumping from
skyscrapers & steering Dodge
            Chargers past motorcycling
        assassins. He was making

a joke, but every time I
        ran into this poet for
the next few days he kept on
            mentioning John Wick & my
        poem as synonymous.

I couldn't tell if this guy
        was trying to insult me, so
I just kept telling him how
           much I admire his work &
        how lucky I felt to read

with him, which I do & I
        did, but I wanted to tell
you this story because on
           the plane ride back home I
        read your new book *The Poetics*

of Wrongness and now I keep
        wondering: what if my poems
are all audio clips from
           bad action movies I've written
        & produced in my head?

What if I'm really every
        role Keanu Reeves ever
played? What if I'm really a
           time travelling stoner on
        the page? What if I'm matrixed

inside intuitive line
        breaks or curtal sonnets
or stepped-septasyllabic
           cinquains as they unfold here?
        What if I'm undercover,

a Fed posing as surfer?
        & why be ridiculous
enough to ask these questions
           in any old poem, let
        alone one that tends toward

the vatic like railroad tracks
        through Whitman's endless vistas?
Because poems don't contain.
                    Because poems don't behave.
        Because to be wrong is to

open your mouth & begin,
        to unquill & uncoil, to
embrace the recoil that will
                inevitably follow
        radical vulnerability.

I am a cis hetero
        white male middle aged middle
class suburban overweight
                American dad. All things
        I shouldn't admit in this

poem. It's true: I spend more
        time listening than I do
speaking, more time reading than
                I do writing. *All I want
        is endless love* & to sing.

But reading you, Rachel, I
        am reminded of Rich &
Rukeyser & Clifton &
                Plath & Sexton & Coleman
        & all the other women

whose words force me to reckon
        with the patriarchies of
sense & structure worrying
                my thoughts into cul-de-sacs
        where ghost-rabbits go unkinged.

Meanwhile, your dictums queen me.
Long poems take time to read.
Time of the hedgehog & gull,
anemone time, time of
barnacle clinging to hull.

Long poems are confessional.
&, of course, I've poured it all
out here—except these words have
little to do with shame or
repentance, but I guess I'm

reaching after a lost grace,
or the idea of such,
as I grapple with this urge
to say & sing & in so
doing to—maybe—understand.

Long poems create intimacy.
They wife you. They husband you.
They spouse you as they espouse.
They wed us to a single
lineation of sunlight

coming from the far door as
the dying calf genuflects
to its mother. *Long poems
are "about" something; long poems
are about nothing but themselves.*

This one is about itself
& about the nature of
the long poem & poems
in general & the poems
of Harvey Hix & about

all the things I want to say
        to my kids & my wife &
my mother & my brother
                & my friends & to you, dear
        reader, stranger, co-author

of the version of myself
        spinning through these stepped cinquains.
Long poems discover themselves.
                They keep coming to themselves
        in the dark woods of their own

journeywork. That is to say,
        they keep encountering, still;
they embody the stillness
                of becoming, which is rain
        tapping on a temple roof.

Long poems are ambitious.
        They gesture at the epic.
They also bleat the question,
                "Who cares what I have to say?"
        & answer anyway with more

than the ego's bell jar, the clang
        of some divine Liberty
Bell cracked with competing tropes
                of nation & need & dream.
        Long poems humble the poet

because the poet exposes
        more of herself. I am here,
I am saying, you know what
                I mean. I get so much wrong.
        I prove that I'm merely an

animal unfolding in
      one eternal instant, whose
muzzle nudges against the white
          space of the page, & who paws
      the air, running in his sleep.

xiii. (Rational Numbers)

As a teenager, & then,
      as a young adult, I was
always laddering up the
         anger inside me, always
    courting the irrational.

I rejected the logic
      of dogwood & iris, &
the anticipation of
        cornflower's blue, rejected
    integer & timetable.

I uncoupled myself from
      common denominator
& the attempt to solve for
        X, rejected the blueprints
    & theorems of the final

solution, rejected drone
      strike, the napalm of AI,
& surveillance capital,
        rejected all isms except
    neologism as prophet

against empire, as religion
            of the unsayable said,
as eternity in the gut
                        of the ampersand, event
            horizon of period,

semicolon's comet &
            moon, the electrons circling
the colon, the cliff's edge of em-
                        dash seared into the daydreams
            of an infant coinage's

first cry. & now my angers
            have fled. They have been worked out
longhand in the glad maths
                        of that grand slow distraction,
            parenthood. & now I tie

my daughter's ballet slippers
            too tight, & retie them so
she can jeté the living
                        room, a streak of sunlight struck
            & frozen above the hardwood.

My son, almost two years old,
            holds the toy phone to his ear
& pretends to talk to me.
                        He squeals as his sister leaps
            in front of him & I think

as I sit on the couch next to
            my wife, the dog curled between
us, this is all I'll ever have
                        of heaven. This is all one
            could want for an afterlife.

& yet I'm keenly aware of
     the kinds of violence that tend
& engender this safety,
        the shorthand of shackle &
     pledge & originalism,

Founding Fathers dividing
     & multiplying within
each one of us, redcoats lined
        up to volley at the stars
     inside the flag as it flaps

along the palisades of
     the fortress we've erected
from woodbine & redwing &
        fey glade in the middle of
     an endless mythic forest.

Meanwhile, the unceded land
     goes unacknowledged, treaties
written on buck hides dyed blue
        hang in the courthouse, & I
     wait for ladybugs to swarm

my hands outstretched in the form
     of this long poem, spindle
of my hope, tether to this
        Earth dwarfed by the expanding
     universe contained in cell

& organ & fingertip
     tapping out the anthem of
a bespoke nation I keep
        in a cage in my chest with
     two doves & a sick eagle.

xiv. (Shadows of Houses)

Harvey, I'm lost in the throes
        of this long poem, longing
for the ping aluminum
            bats make in the ballpark dusk,
        longing for the music of

cricket & lawnmower &
        stick in the spokes of my bike
& the wind kissing my face
            as I coast downhill no hands,
        my little brother there too,

cycling beside me into
        the separate futures we now
inhabit & wobble through,
           leaving far behind the paths
        we blazed through the underbrush,

the plywood ramps we once made,
        long decomposed & fused to
nutrient shooting up stems
            & tendrils of wildflower
        & poison ivy itself

long wilted & rotted &
          cycling through soil & seedpod,
summer after summer gone
                    past without remark, without
          adventure, with new sets of

brothers & sisters cycling
          along. Here I go again,
losing myself to find some
                    other strand to pick up &
          follow to its conclusion.

As an undergraduate,
          my brother studied Nietzsche
& Kant, & we were always
                    discussing the eternal
          return & Zarathustra

always enjoining us to
          abide here & to love this
ever unfolding instant,
                    to refuse to revise this
          long poem, but to stutter

it out into the abyss
          inside you, which is inside
me, to instead coast downhill,
                    no hands, the wind kissing you
          hard on the mouth, partnering

you on your parallel track,
          toward a ramp the size of
an Olympic ski jump &
                    as you take flight to wonder
          about the *Groundwork*, those hours

the categorical im-
            perative weighed into us,
as we hiked the trails above
                        Salt Springs State Park & smoked weed
            in the twilight of the gods,

or so the THC would
            tell us, shotgunning from blunt
to throat to lung, imploding
                        in a mushroom cloud of thought
            hop frogging thought after thought.

The problem with the impulse
            to universalize is
that it—that it—turns into
                        one THAT which should stay many,
            the selves & unselves that make

the congregation of want
            & need & sperm & the light
at the end of the tunnel
                        of the fallopian tube
            where the nimbus of egg lights

the multiverse of the self
            before it even gets started.
Even then, the din of play-
                        ground & cafeteria
            & classroom & field & woods

& neighborhood & alley
            & overpass & office
& court & the quiet of
                        a lonely teenage bedroom
            & the nights & afternoons

in the marriage bed with its
       throbs & thrusts & its love groans
winnowing out the window
           the chaff of the lonesomeness
      of existence in one silk

single ecstatic string of
       sighs of you as she & he
untether in this fullness,
          this abundance of curve &
     heft & come & come & come.

iv. (God Bless)

How strange, Harvey, to move from
      bike riding through the suburbs
to metaphysics, morals,
            sex, & death, but I guess this
      is always the arc, & how

profound that all of this keeps
      unfolding in the ark of
a single moment, which is this
            poem, my lifespan, my last &
      first breath braiding together.

Harvey you said, "Our country
      has taken a course, especially
in foreign policy, that
            I find troubling, & that shows
      up in my life as a perceived

need to apologize to
      friends overseas when I
correspond with them, & as
            a growing realization
      that I've been a free rider

enjoying the benefits
        of the circumstances I
was born into, without always
            taking responsibility
        for their consequences." & that

in a book where you braid Bush
        & bin Laden together
into the striations of
            a poetic discourse that
        questions the very nature

of poetry & poemness,
        as so many poems do.
Is that the point, or a point?
            That the line between poem
        & nonpoem is no line

at all, like the line between
        president & terrorist?
That to categorize is
            to lose sight? Hybridity
        as sigil & origin?

I'm writing this twenty years
        after the start of the war
in Iraq (the second one).
            On the news, Tammy Duckworth,
        the senator & vet (D-

Ill.), answers a question
        about her injuries: "My
sacrifice is for the Con-
            stitution, & that is always
        worth it." The congressman with

the eyepatch (R-Texas) agrees
        the war was: "a time in my
life that I don't regret for
        a second, even with the
        missing eye." Harvey, I keep

dreaming phantom limbs burning
        the constitution & dead
Iraqi children leaving trails
        of blood in the corridors
        of Walter Reed & on rides

at Disney World. I'm thinking
        about the young woman who
spoke at the writing panel
        for female war veterans,
        the scar on her neck where she

was shot outside Ramadi
        rising and falling as she talked
about her fellow soldiers
        with a love that rendered moot
        any academic insights

into the nature of war
        & writing & war writing
& witness & disrupting
        the narrative & so on.
        The Constitution is a

scar on the neck & a poem
        is a scar on the neck &
a rising & a falling
        of that scar as a poet
        gives breath to sorrow & love.

Remember, the dead children
        are real & so is the scar
& the scarred hollow socket
           behind the congressman's black
       eyepatch is real as any

nebula in deep space.
       George W. Bush paints pictures
in his retirement. He's not
         bad, is he? & bin Laden's
     corpse remains clicked & captured

in a Navy SEAL's cell phone,
       another glad assassin
doing the wet work of empire
         with a grin on his face &
     two glints in his two good eyes.

xvi. (Interleaf: To My Brother)

Brother is such a close word,
        a rabbit word, a ghost word,
a throat word, a word of blood
              & root & cell & stem shot
      through concrete, an agree word,

a word belonging to toad
        & gnat alike, a dog word,
a mitochondrial word,
          a rivering outdoor word,
      a toehold near the summit.

Daeman, I feel like I'm always
        arbitraging with the past
& the future, each poem whorled
           with the fingerprints smudging
      a Ken Griffey Jr. rookie

card in a cigar box from
        grandpa's house & holding out
the halogen light of some
           final hospital room I
      hopefully won't find myself

in before my last breath pines
        across the waters into
a purple the shade of mom's
            dresses when we lived in the
    army green apartment house

in Schenectady, our bunk-
        bed a rowboat we steered each
night as mom & dad fought or
            made love in the next room. I
    wish I could remember what

we talked about all those nights
        before fading off into
chiaroscuro slumbers,
            the aquatics of sleep usurping
    our separate common futures.

 What illusory brindled
        beast writhes there in the shadows?
 I want to think we discussed
            the shades of perennials
    in grandmother's flowerbeds,

but I'm sure our talk was more
        delinquent & innocent,
imbued with the nightlights of
            baseball diamonds & the smell
    of fresh cut grass caroming

through chain link fences from park
        to lawn to side street to ave.
& back through the bitter cul-
            de-sacs of the suburban
    dark, back to me dreaming you

into a poem where you are
              holding your newborn daughter
in a photograph with big
                      mountains looming behind you,
              into your niece & nephew

pretending you live in our
              attic, as they shout "Uncle
Daeman" at the ceiling fan
                      & I repeat the refrain:
              brother is such a far word,

an orbital word, a train
              of stars from the hem of night,
a word that wrestles other
                      words to the ground in front of
              a Denny's at 2 A.M..

xvii. (The Gospel)

Harvey, I'm thinking of this
        passage you translated from
the early life of Jesus:
            "Walking once with *xer* mother
        across the city square, Jesus

saw a teacher teaching some
        children. Twelve sparrows flurried
down from the wall, bickering,
           & tumbled into the teacher's
        lap. Seeing this, Jesus laughed.

The teacher, noticing *xer*
        laugh, was filled with anger, &
said, What's so funny? Jesus
           replied, Listen, a widow
        is on her way here carrying

what little wheat she can afford,
        but when she gets here she'll stumble
& spill the wheat. These sparrows
           are fighting over how many
        grains each will get. Jesus didn't

leave until what *xe'd* predicted
        had occurred. The teacher, seeing
Jesus' words become accomplished
           deeds, wanted to have *xer* run
      out of town, along with *xer*

mother." Jesus as trickster,
      as full participant in
the gentle follies that make
          up a life, as traveler
      unstuck in geography

& era, as metaphor
      for the way time is always
unfolding & refolding
          around us, how an hour is
      each instant in it at once.

Right now, I'm laughing at words
      that will alight on the lines
of this poem, the words that
          are bickering now over
      the wheat to come, the ones I've

winnowed & spilled already
      in a remembered future
hovering just beyond
          the vowel of this moment.
      The words of this poem are

sparrows & widows & grains
      spilled & accidents & endless
laughter from the throat of a
          preteen God walking the wings
      of the vast squabbling unseen.

xvii. (Demonstrategy)

& what is that preteen God
        really doing? Committing
to mystery. Priesting dark
            & undark alike with mirth.
        Choosing the guffaw instead

of the sermon or the sword.
        Harvey, this poem commits
itself to mystery, it
            rejects the bettering pulse
        of short poems written for

journals, MFA workshops,
        hip reading series. It says:
"in poetry, the ideal
            is not *given*, but ever *at stake*."
        So much & so little is

at stake here. My whole life is
        an atom, a grain of wheat spilled
two millennia ago,
            the mirror of the lives of
        my parents & my children,

a revolving door that leads
          into an opulent hall
I'll never step foot in, words
                    strung together like ruby
          progressions of taillights in

a C.D. Wright poem, drawn
          heart anatomically
correct on the cover of
                    an outlaw country album
          lost in an unborn grandchild's

attic a century from
          now. I wonder how many
generations of family
                    will read my words once they've died
          in the pulp of a handful

of poetry presses. My
          ambition: to echo in
the hearts of my daughter
                    & my son as they stumble
          through orchard & overpass.

Though I return to your words,
          Harvey, and sing from there: "My
shoes subsidize child labor
                    in Singapore, the car I
          drive sanctions the circumstances

in which female factory
          workers are routinely raped
& killed at the U.S./Mex-
                    ico border, my trash is
          dumped into a vast dead zone

in the Pacific, & on
   & on." & on & on &
on, except perhaps in poems,
   which resist, or exist as
  gifts, outside the abattoirs

of Capital & other
   -isms. In poems, we might
be & become our own gods
   & grammars, noticing an
  aspect of an *is*ness that

isn't only or any
   ours, but which has moved somehow
into the profoundly other
   ours of hours after hours of
  a doppelgänger face pressed

against the cube of the page,
   like some wild bergamot &
blue verbena pressed between
   the yellowing leaves of *Deep-*
step Come Shining one hundred

years hence, those preserved petals
   turned to artifact of wind
& rain & sunlight & dirt
   & the communion of stem
  & seed & sprouting skyward.

xix. (How It Is that We)

The opening pages of
          How It Is that We sprout sky-
ward, dare our anesthetic
                    cosmos to tickle up some
          confirmation of mission

& purpose in the world out-
          side compromised bisected
sonnets jawing their logic
                    to the lessons of rainstorms
          in black & white cinema.

I keep funneling back to
          the beautiful faces in
Japanese samurai films
                    from the fifties and sixties,
          contorted in pain & glee

& attention & valor
          & bravado & grief
& every other shade of
                    moonlight on ripples of want
          & dream & reel & play dead.

Those swift emotive faces
        call to something fragile in
me, the stem of a glass rose
            splintering into treble
        clefs for the cellos my lungs

are tempted to abscond with—
        what I'm trying to say is
something about the image,
            how it accrues musics as
        it travels within oneself,

how all I can't unsee re-
        psalms itself inside me as
I go about my days &
            perfects the pitch of its hum
        & hymn before it escapes,

as the words I write & speak
        rewrite me & read me back
from the teleprompter of
            the self, the vast storehouse of
        the human mind filled with half-

finished heavens & bits of
        dialogue cadged from the throats
of old character actors
            I can recognize, but not
        name, the friends lost in the past,

the absences I refuse
        to grasp at over touchscreen
after touchscreen. It is strange
            to think of how much sorrow
        & violence & ardor

I carry around with me
            as a viewer. How it is
that Tony Montana has died
                    more than a dozen times in
            front of my eyes only to

rise again along with his
            overwrought Cuban accent.
He's alive there, enacting
                    his inverted form of Greek
            tragedy forever, brought

low by a momentary
            lapse into goodness, reverse
harmatia of second thoughts,
                    causing him to foil the car
            bombing that would have killed kids.

How it is never the plot
            that matters, but something wedged
between the narrative &
                    the image that finally
            tinctures into poetry.

xx. (Interleaf: To Gerard Manley Hopkins)

I imagine your corpse unlike
     that of the nun recently
disinterred in Missouri,
          her flesh fragrant & barely
     decomposed, her cadaver

pronounced a miraculous
     wedge & relic between the worlds
of life & death. Your body,
          Gerard, loveliest of men,
     most angelic of poets,

molders underground, wedlocked
     to dust & decay & etched
with echoes of raucous unsound,
          blaring of bone & sinew
     & vein fused in one quelled call,

clarion of nothingness,
     beyond the last eyelash dunned
into dirt, unstrung from ash
          & ember & inscaped spark
     of minutequick existence.

The mitochondria in
      each one of my cells call out
each to each & to you too
        & to the space where you should
     be & once were & are now

gashing gold vermillion, smeared,
      teared, tiered, trod, grappling in gray
with the holy ghost of a word
       made flush with the sloe-juice of
     these phonemes tumbling away

from the wrecks & waves in me
     & in you & in this poem,
which is cohabitating
     with the great pang of a felled
       ash tree forever maimed in

the little low heaven of
     the Everest arcing spine
of your spiritself strengthwraithed
       in each every last lushlash
     of your pen, dappling dawn in

your journal. Gerard, I've been
     living in your words for more
than two decades & you have
       been & become bonepledged since
     the first flip of a page in

the Dover Thrift Edition
     I bought at nineteen, your words
fresh fire coal chestnut falling
       through the mortal trash of this
     tumbling to decay I've booned

& brightened into, this life,
       everlastingness of earthless
roughcast heaven-roistering,
          whim hymned against the blueblack
     blank of death & its errant

obscure apt punctuations,
       its idiosyncratic
capitalizations &
          apostrophes selfwrung &
     hung on dissevered dots of

a pointillist still life of
       unnamed asterisms coat racked
throughout the Milky Way &
          forming our constellations
     as seen from Andromeda.

I see the Andromeda
       galaxy in you, Gerard,
its spiral burred to blurring,
          its course set for collision
     with the pocket universe

inside the mandible of
       an ant, inside the ink of
Einstein's famous formula,
          after the prehistoric
     pigments in dragonfly wings.

& I ask you to instress
       the feeling diamond drawn deep
in every poem you've inscribed
          on my capillaries &
     arteries & turn the chrism

of your music into one
         word my son can say with joy,
the way at two he repeats:
                 "purple" "yo-yo," "Barbara,"
         & "Grogu," as if each word

held the key to the meaning
         of life, which each does, if life's
meaning has something to do
                 with how a son summons song
         & sweetness enough for his

family & builds from there
         a poem in his father's
throat & lungs & ribcage &
                 heart, a poem cribbed from your
         morning kingdoms praised past change

& transmitted via gene,
         from sperm to egg to zygote
to fetus to newborn to
                 squalling to tantrum to word
         to eardrum homed to bloodstream

& thus from father to son
         & back to father. & from
father (me) back to this page,
                 this poem leaving me sprung
         into the mind & heart of

whomever you are, reading
         these lines, or hearing these words
& ordering them under
                 your eyelids & in your nerves,
         orbiting your cochlea

on their way to the neurons
      firing in your brain, axon
& dendrite & soma lit
          with an electric whiplash
      that repeats: *this is, this is*—

Gerard, you are not nothing
      now & I hope to one day
share that fate, to be eons
          inside the spines of a book
      reprinted & reprinted

& read & reread, to be,
      to become a poem once
& indefinitely &
          perpetually to be
      carried in the heart of kin

& unkin alike until
      time ceases to time itself
inside you in increments
          & instead you coast inside
      one long dappled dawning Now

with no after & before,
      with just the quick-finned & quilled
& unassailable strange
          fickle freckled swift slow sour
      adazzle dim dreck of *this is,*

this is, this is, shing like shook
      foil, like the glint in the eye
of kingfisher & kestrel
          & thrush & plover, while *this*
      is shaped clouds float overhead,

& the sun is the sun dreamed
        by my son in utero
& I am him & my own
            father & mother arming
        me with sorrow & trying

to pass on only light for
        him & for his sister, fey
bookends for my body of
            work, which is my life chirping:
        this is, yes, Gerard, *this is*—

xxi. (Incident Light)

this is, Harvey, insistent,
   the incident light of *this*
is, pulsing, dithyrambic,
     alive: "I take my troubles
  scribbled, not erased." This is.

The absences accumulate.
    Like blowflies. Bougainvillea.
The debris at the bottom
     of the lake: old snowmobiles
  that have come to resemble

sunken galleons you dream
   in a lucid dream where you
dive through the murk, knifing
     your way through the depths of *this*
  is, shook to shining again

& again, awakening
   on the verge of fathoming,
literally fathoming,
    the below of, the beyond
  of, the belong of what's gone.

Poetry is elegy,
       fast forwarded or rewound,
returning late or sooner,
              or just turning like a spit
       of pierced & seared chicken hearts

at a Brazilian steak-
       house, ready for you to chomp
down on the tiniest one,
              & so, to ingest the strength
       of a hundred hundred hens.

 Life's so strange & so is this
       poem, roasting in its own
juices, aware "what is real
              is experienced in im-
       pulse" & we always mean some-

thing other than what we meant
       to mean. I'm typing up my
troubles now, instead of down
              jotting them or scribbling them
       sideways into the margins.

What is real in a poem
       is experienced as pulse;
how you get to two fingers
              on a wrist & counting out
       heartbeats is all in the line-

breaks. *This I knew before I*
       knew anything else: I needed
some richer way to see, a
              cape of flame, a ribbon of
       ash, the whole last century,

its concentration camps &
         atom bombs & squabbles of
bone & whiteness & its sharp
                  teeth. Hold this poem to your
         ear. Hear it saying the sea.

xxii. (I'm Here to Learn to Dream in Your Language)

Listen to this poem say
        the sea in not so many
words. Listen to the meter
            of its waves enjambed against
        the rocky shoreline of self

& unself. I'm here to learn
        to dream in your language, dear
reader. I'm here to unlearn
            the language of waking, which
        is what poetry is meant

for, this kind of unlearning
        that leads into a deeper
dream of words below the words,
            beyond the phonics that yawns
        like a hibernating bear

in the convex mirror of
        a brain, yours or mine yawning
amidst the brushfires of time.
            What kind of cosmos must this
        cosmos be, to laugh at us

like this? To let us burn like
            redwoods ablaze? For sirens
to cry into us? To let
                us be pried apart, unhinged,
            immolated in God's name?

To mix our metaphors with
            the mass extinction event
we are all living through, or
                better yet, dying through,
            upstate New York enveloped

in Canadian wildfire
            smoke as I write this, my lungs
& nostrils filled with a smell
                that reminds me of incense
            during the high holy days

when I was an altar boy,
            more than three decades ago,
back when I believed in God,
                the god of immolation
            & atom bomb, the god of

my parents' multiplying
            fears & angers & sorrows,
god whose acolytes & priests
                were pedophiles, rapists,
            & at their best, thieves of joy.

I reject The Church, any
            altar or attar or balm
outside the wilderness of
                the self. I reject the thought
            of apocalypse, its hand-

servants & disciples, its plagues
        & horsemen & the vague tropes
of its endless rehearsals.
                A man in love curves through the
        above, the way a whale rills

through the below, slow as
        though lumbering, but so wholly,
with so whole a body, hummed
             forth in the depths calling out
        in clicks & whistles & swells

below the surface a wave-
        fracturing radiant *this*
is—I embrace my wife, my
             children, my dog, & you, dear
        reader, whomever you are.

I embrace you & reject
        all that isn't music, all
dovetailing trauma & its
        aftermaths. I love being
            alive inside this lintel

of light & leaving with all
        its twinges & promises
burrowing into me &
            quitting me without taking
        the innate tenderness I

feel ballooning up in me
        at almost every moment—
call it gratitude this breadth,
            this extensiveness meadowed
        in me, hammocked in me now.

I could say of this poem:
      "What began as mingle be-
came bump up against." *Somewhere*
          a universe compound of
     circles spins, effortlessly.

xxiii. (The Death of H.L. Hix)

There's nothing I want more than
       to be alive on the page.
Elsewhere, Harvey, I said to
          you: To live a life in
poetry, for me, is to

be after this loosening,
       to be a votary of
this release, to praise the space
          where page meets flesh. As you say
       in *Demonstrategy*: "in

poetry the ideal is
       not *given*, but ever at
stake." Cyclical re-staking.
          Infinite becoming. Faith.
       To loosen reality's

hold. To break the dam & let
       life flood into the lyric
& the lyric flood into
          life. To see no place that is
       not song, & so, to see no

place not made vibrant with change.
      Harvey, I'm vibrant with this
paragraph from your novel:
            "H.L. Hix had not expect-
            ed his life to go the way

everyone else's life
      goes, & in that expecta-
tion he had been just like eve-
            ryone else, since no one thinks
            their life will go the way eve-

ryone else's goes, until
      it has gone that way. Every-
thing that happened in H.L.
            Hix's life had felt to him
            unique & exclusive; in

this, it was just like, every-
      thing that happens in every-
one else's life." Except I
            distrust this version of you,
            & I wonder what it means

for a life to go one way
      or another, & having
gone, to find the paths that run
            parallel & intersect,
            worn really about the same

like those famous misprisioned
      roads in Frost. That way lies all
sighs & ages & ages
            hence. This is how your novel
            falls away from the corruptions

of reality: letting
        cynicism & irony
exsanguinate the prose
            of its lyric blood. & then
        toward the end after H.

L. Hix in fictive form has
        evanesced—almost—there's this:
"H. L. Hix's death like eve-
            ry death before his & eve-
        ry death to follow, was a

fate worse than death. His depar-
        ture was absolute, absent-
ing himself utterly, but
            without at all compromis-
        ing the wholeness of the whole.

His no longer *being* did
        not make anything else no
longer itself. His no long-
            er *being* did not one whit
        diminish Being. *His* un-

iverse was taken from
        him fully & finally:
nothing for him to exper-
            ience, no *him* to exper-
        ience it. *The* universe

remained the universe, the
        wholeness of the whole no less
whole for having excluded
            him, the nothingness of no-
        thingness no less nothing for

having subsumed him." Reading this
        I think, yes, & *this is* &
everything & nothing in
                between the molecules that
        compose the visible &

invisible worlds. This is.
        I'm coasting on a quark in
a hadron collider. I'm
                the tiniest electric
        charge in the known multiverse.

All I have is words & their
        textures & tastes, sacrosanct
meteorites bombarding
                the surface of a future
        no less whole for my having

been excluded bodily
        from it, my books & poems
a series of archways where
                my children & their children
        might glimpse the nonesuch of me

& know what I was trying to
        do was to sing myself back
& forth in the hammock of
                my life as a stone skipping
        through the generations of

my family tree, upon
        the roots of which I pour out
a domestic beer & sing
                an anthem for the dead &
        doomed & dying I carry

in my heart, in my heartbeat,
  in my heartache, in the break
of a leaf stem jammed between
    stone, breaking without sound, I
  carry you, my loves, my loves.

xxiv. (Flyleaf: To My Children & To My Children's Children)

My loves, my loves, my loves, we
        have so much & too little
time together here on Earth.
                We dawdle in a garden
        in a William Blake poem

as I try & I try to
        learn & to teach you how to
carry the beams of love, which are
                so heavy, so light, they phase in
        & out of touch & weight as

we heft them with their gangly
        implications, their Christs killed
& rising from the tombs on
                infinite variations
        of our humble planet Earth.

I've noticed the word "Earth" has
        recurred in this long poem
more often than it does in
                most of my work, & maybe
        that's because I'm after toes

in the soil here like when I
              watch you play with your dump trucks
in the front yard & you dig
                            up the sod & sift the dirt
              through your hands & hold the rocks

& pebbles up & make them
              talk like dolls made of stone with
the small squeakiest voices
                            like cartoon voles singing out
              from the mouths of their burrows.

We are in this era, my loves,
              my lovely little ones, when
everything sings & each day
                            your mother & I & you
              two & the dog are in

this elaborate production
              called childhood & it is so
magic to be there with you
                            as you dance to Disney songs
              in the living room & change

costumes to become a witch
              & a vampire & a prince
& a princess & a cop
                            & a cowgirl & a knight
              & a caballero queen

& king of our humble home
              with your crayoned fire blazing
on the dining room walls &
                            your pictures hung up with scotch
              tape & rainbow masking tape

at adult eye level &
       the spritely way you both walk,
you my daughter, lilac wraith
          fey & flourishing, & you,
     my son, tender smiley gnome

of my heart & so much un-
       knowing. When you two waylay
me & pull my beard & put
          bows on my head & climb all
     over me when I sit beside

you, sadness voyages far
       away & paradise cracks
open my ribcage & plants
          itself in the four chambers
     of the red studio that

houses my dreams for you &
       pumps blood throughout my body,
which is the *this is* the world
          sieves through to me & from which
     I wonder: am I a shell?

a machine for processing
       words & sensation, network
of electrical impulses
          misfiring alongside you?
     No. No answer. Whatever

this is, I'm grateful for it.
       I revere the dark that book-
ends a life. I've come to see
          my being, all Being, as
     a forever composed of

Nows, as Dickinson wrote on
       an envelope she never
mailed. & the Nows of this are
           not some hiccupping series
      of constellated feelings.

The Nows are instead one Now
       seen from every side, inside
& out & from dimensions
           beyond my understanding,
      like charting Stephen Hawking's

by scoring it with a lone
       note from Coltrane's horn as he
doodles eternity in
           an unreleased outtake stashed
      away, but intuited

by the very existence
       of joy & shrieking grief &
the stillness of certain types
           of punctuation, commas,
      for instance, as the speedbumps

& false eyelashes of truth,
       schooling the flighty pupils
of her eyes, turbulent &
           wanton & sucking the pulp
      from a Florida orange.

Dear children, I'm imagining
       you both as elderly, as
thirty years older than I am
           as I write this, as having
      lived most of your life & still,

I hope, as carrying your
        mother & me in your hearts.
I'm imagining all you've seen
            & all the pains I would take
        from you if I could & I'm

imagining your children
        & all the things they've seen &
all the pain you'd take from them
            if you could & I'm hoping
        that your lives were filled with more

happiness & ease than with
        sorrow & I'm daggering
myself by imagining
            the moments you both blink out
        of existence, & your kids

carrying you in their hearts
        through disaster & disease
& I am hoping these words
            will sing to the kernel of
        you both bonded to the bones

of whomever descends from
        us: there is a heaven in
these days when you are very
            young & we can gather it
        to us & dwell in it for-

ever, dancing the simple
        truth of *this is* & *this is*
& *this is*, this love this sweet
            swift Eden yawning out in
        all directions, toddling

past linear conceptions
        of time, sprawling lanky Nows
of daughter & son, mother
                & father, sibling & parent,
        spouse & friend gamboling

like sunlight & moonlight in
        the meadows of a shared heart-
land, landing like a single
                ladybug on a wedding
        dress your mother will dance in

& did—once & after all
        & always yonder, ever
edging into the inch of
                us, the saying of us, she,
        the readers, the dancers, you.

Acknowledgments

Thank you to the editors and staff of the following publications in which sections of this work have appeared, sometimes in different versions: *Copper Nickel* and *Rattle*. "To My Brother" was selected as a finalist for the 2024 *Rattle* Poetry Prize.

Thank you to the staff of Bordighera Press, especially Nicholas Grosso, Fred Gardaphé, and Anthony Tamburri.

Thank you to Philip Brady and Robert Mooney, for putting me into dialogue with my heroes, H.L. Hix and William Heyen.

Thank you to my friends, family, teachers, and students—too numerous to name, but a partial list of which includes: Maria Mazziotti Gillan, Liz Rosenberg, Joe Weil, Paul-William Burch, Karin Terrebessey, Salvador Fajardo, Leah Umansky, Nicole Santalucia, Deanna Dorangrichia, Abby Murray, Amy Smith, Adam Gellings, Nathan Lipps, Tom Bouman, Nat Bouman, Emily Bouman, Katherine Bouman, Murray Silverstein, Gerald Fleming, Lynne Knight, Tony Bianco, Matt Martel, Paul Keida, Tera Buckley, Liz Denman, Shelly Sellepack, Jon Morris, Marella Feltrin-Morris, Faisal Mohyuddin, Stephen "Birddog" Blabac, and Christian Teresi.

In memory of Jason Shinder and Joe Salerno, poets who died too young.

Thank you to Charity Kittler, Kate Northrop and William Heyen.

Thank you to Harvey, for the friendship and the poetry.

Thank you to mom and Daeman, for the encouragement, support, and understanding.

Thank you to my wife Christina, who enables and inspires my life in poetry.

Thank you to my children, for the radiance.

Lastly, thank you to anyone who reads this book.

Notes

H. L. Hix was born in Oklahoma in 1960 and raised in various small towns in the south. After earning his B.A. from Belmont College (now Belmont University) and his Ph.D. (in philosophy) from the University of Texas, Hix taught at the Kansas City Art Institute and was an administrator at the Cleveland Institute of Art, before joining the faculty of the University of Wyoming, where, after a term as director of the creative writing MFA, he now teaches in the Philosophy Department and the Creative Writing Program.

Shortly before my second book, *Ill Angels* (Etruscan Press, 2019), was published, a letter from Wyoming appeared in my mailbox. It was a note from Harvey, congratulating me on the book. Thus began our epistolary friendship. Later, Etruscan Press published a volume, featuring collections by Hix, William Heyen, and I. Over the last six years I have come to regard H.L. Hix as one of the greatest contemporary American poets, as the most wildly innovative and the most philosophically complex, and as a compadre living a life in poetry.

This poem is written in stepped-septasyllabic cinquains, a stanzaic pattern I developed and used in my book *Midwhistle* (University of Wisconsin Press, 2023). The stanzaic pattern was inspired by William Heyen's advice and by his book, *To William Merwin* (Mammoth Books, 2007). This book is a sequel of sorts to *Midwhistle*. I hope to write a third book eventually and turn this into a trilogy. Each section of this book (aside from the prologue, interleaves, and flyleaf), shares a title with a book written, translated, or edited by H.L. Hix.

Prologue (Leaflet: To Marie Howe Here on Earth and to Jason Shinder in the Crystalline Sphere of Dante's *Paradiso*, Canto XXVII) Marie Howe (born 1950) is one of the greatest living American poets. Her friend, Jason Shinder (1955–2008), authored three miraculous books of poetry. Shinder was fond of quoting Blake's famous lines: "And we are put on earth a little space, / That we may learn to bear the beams of love." In Canto XXVII, Dante encounters, among other things, what John D. Sinclair calls "the boundary of space and time, of all the created universe that is relative and subject to change."

i. (Rain Inscription) The leading question of *Rain Inscription* (Etruscan Press, 2017)—How should I live? —initiates this profoundly lustrous and elusive exploration of our bodies (of work, at work, and otherwise). This is my second favorite H.L. Hix book.

ii. (As Easy As Lying) *As Easy As Lying: Essays on Poetry* (Etruscan Press, 2002) explores the terrain of late 20th and early 21st century American poetry with great erudition. Simply speaking, the essays in this volume reiterate the intertwined questions: 1) what do poets do? and 2) what are poems for? These are questions at the heart of Hix's oeuvre.

iii. (Legible Heavens) *Legible Heavens* (Etruscan Press, 2008) translates portions of the Bible and the apocrypha as it examines notions of the divine in the mundane and works to transcribe the paradise that can only be apprehended in the periphery of lyric saying.

iv. (Interleaf: To My Dead Father) Dominic Di Stefano Jr. (1946-2013) was my father: a career postal worker, US Army veteran, devout Catholic, cancer victim, and lover of the poetry of Emily Dickinson.

v. (Lines of Inquiry) *Lines of Inquiry* (Etruscan Press, 2011) was the first book of Harvey's I read seriously and deeply, before I began corresponding with him. It is also the book where I first read the Harold Bloom quote with which he blurbed this book. *Lines of Inquiry* is a truly radical hybridization of poetry and literary criticism. This is the book that allowed me to see that each poem I write is an act of literary criticism and that literary criticism can be poetry.

vi. (Perfect Hell) Published the year I graduated from high school, *Perfect Hell* (Gibbs Smith, 1996) is Harvey's debut collection. Each poem in this book takes its title from a quote by a philosopher, a poet, or a writer. Hix's long exploration of intertextuality and poetry-as-philosophy begins here.

vii. (American Anger) In the disclaimers at the end of *American Anger* (Etruscan Press, 2015), Hix notes that the preceding volume is a threnody for the "numberless casualties of American anger" and that he sees this book as an abstract for an indefinitely larger work. I see it as an attempt to situate the H.L. Hix composed through, and dwelling in, his oeuvre between the poles of American violence and American poetry. This is Hix at his most Blakean, offering to illuminate the imperial and tyrannical aspects of legal, lyrical, and political discourse.

viii. (Interleaf: To My Living Mother) Donna Di Stefano (born 1952) is my mother: orphan, foster child, housewife, decades long state university employee, convert to Catholicism, Director of Religious Education for Saint Mary of the Assumption Church, fierce supporter of her sons, and grandmother.

In a brilliant essay from *Pig Notes & Dumb Music: Prose on Poetry* (Boa Editions, 1998), William Heyen writes that perhaps the most beautiful line of poetry ever written is Whitman's line from "The Sleepers": "The white hair of the mother shines on the white wrist of the daughter."

ix. (First Fire, Then Birds) *First Fire, Then Birds: Obsessionals 1985-2000* (Etruscan Press, 2010) reimagines what a *New and Selected* can be, reformulating this convention of the publishing world as a space to transform, rather than to transcribe, a body of work.

x. (Chromatic) *Chromatic* (Etruscan Press, 2006), a finalist for the National Book Award, uses the music of poetry to examine the human desire to dwell in the music of music.

A Love Supreme is John Coltrane's masterwork from 1965. This is my favorite piece of music.

Shoah Train (Etruscan Press, 2003), another National Book Award finalist, is William Heyen's Holocaust opus.

"Misrepresented People" is a song by Stevie Wonder, released on the soundtrack to Spike Lee's *Bamboozled* (2000). Inspired by Wonder's song, I edited an anthology of political poetry titled *Misrepresented People* (NYQ Books, 2018).

xi. (Counterclaims) *Counterclaims: Poets and Poetries Talking Back* (Dalkey Archive Press, 2020) is an anthology project edited by Hix, featuring responses by contemporary poets to Auden's statement: "poetry makes nothing happen" and to Adorno's claim: "to write poetry after Auschwitz is barbaric." In the "Overture," which prefaces the book, Hix writes: "I cling to what is slipping away, *not* so that it will not slip away, but so that I *will*."

xii. (Interleaf: To Rachel Zucker) Rachel Zucker's *The Poetics of Wrongness* (Wave Books, 2023) provides the greatest insight into long poems I have ever read. Zucker's book also made me examine deep patriarchal structures inside myself and to think about how those structures affect my reading and writing life.

xiii. (Rational Numbers) *Rational Numbers* (Truman State University Press, 2000) was selected by Dana Gioia as the winner of the T.S. Eliot prize. The two sections of this book ask the same question in different ways: what am I supposed to do with the knowledge that I will one day die?

xiv. (Shadows of Houses) *Shadows of Houses* (Etruscan Press, 2005) contains some of the most gorgeous lyric poetry of the 21st century. This book is as good, or better than any book of American poetry written in the last hundred years, or ever. My copy, purchased in a used bookstore, is signed by Hix, with a quote from Nietzsche: "Thoughts are the shadows of our feelings—always darker, emptier, and simpler." *Shadows of Houses* is my favorite Hix book.

xv. (God Bless) *God Bless* (Etruscan Press, 2007) repurposes the speeches of George W. Bush and the arguments of Osama bin Laden and weaves those discourses into a lyric dialogue on war and empire. This book also includes interviews with experts on the Middle East, who weigh in on subjects related to 9/11 and "the war on terror."

xvi. (Interleaf: To My Brother) My younger brother, Daeman (born 1980), has always been my best friend, although he might punch me for saying that. When I started seriously writing poetry as an undergraduate, he was my first reader and my first enthusiastic champion. He used to tack my (horrible attempts at) poems to his dorm room walls. Over the years, he has been to many poetry readings. Often, he's the only accountant in the room. My brother and I lead very different lives as adults, separated by geography and the demands of work and family, but I will be forever grateful for our shared childhood and for our wild young adulthood, either despite or because of the occasional wrestling match at Denny's at 2 AM. Daeman, here's another thing to punch me for: I love you.

xvii. (The Gospel) *The Gospel* (Broadstone Books, 2020) integrates the four canonical gospels with dozens of noncanonical apocryphal gospels into a new account of the life of Jesus. Hix's gospel undoes the traditionally masculine gender tilt of the Biblical texts. In Hix's version, the pronouns for God and Jesus are rendered neutral (or plural) to avoid this tilt; "his," for example, is rendered as "xer."

xviii. (Demonstrategy) *Demonstrategy: Poetry, For and Against* (Etruscan Press, 2018) is a book of prose that queries the reasons for and the uses of poetry. Hix provides a labyrinthine excavation of the affirmative and oppositional impulses driving this artform. If you believe, as Clive James wrote, that "a poem is any piece of writing that can't be quoted from except out of context," then *Demonstrategy* is a poem.

xix. (How It Is that We) *How It Is that We* is a kind of rejoinder to, and an elaboration on, *American Anger*, published in *Generations* (Etruscan Press, 2022), a three-in-one volume, which also included William Heyen's *The Nazi Patrol*, and my third book, *Lullaby with Incendiary Device*.

xx. (Interleaf: To Gerard Manley Hopkins) Gerard Manley Hopkins (1844—1889), the English Jesuit priest and formal innovator, is my favorite poet. The dollar that I spent on a whim, to buy the Dover Thrift Edition collection that introduced me to his work when I was nineteen, was the best money I ever spent. Reading his over-the-top alliteration, hurdling his wild portmanteaus, learning the instress and inscape of his metaphors as pulse and breath, and galloping along his sprung rhythms caused me to fall hopelessly and endlessly in love with poetry. I still read him nearly every day.

xxi. (Incident Light) *Incident Light* (Etruscan Press, 2009) explores identity through the biography of Petra Soesemann. In the section titled, "*Night Watch*," Hix's Soesemann relates: "What perceptions I trust defy perspective. / I take my troubles scribbled, not erased."

xxii. (I'm Here to Learn to Dream in Your Language) *I'm Here to Learn to Dream in Your Language* (Etruscan Press, 2015) translates the idiosyncratic logic of the imagination and the subconscious into a lyric examination of spiritual and physical longing.

xxiii. (The Death of H.L. Hix) Harvey sent me *The Death of H.L. Hix* (Serving House Books, 2021) with this note: "I hope you will enjoy poor H.L. Hix's untimely demise." This entertaining novel pays homage to, and parodies Tolstoy's *The Death of Ivan Ilyich.* Hix's novel engages the same fundamental questions underwriting his poetry, questions about reading, writing, meaning, and being.

xxiv. (Flyleaf: To My Children & To My Children's Children) My radiant hearts, Luciana Jubilee Di Stefano (born January 9, 2018) and Dante Natale Di Stefano Jr. (born August 4, 2021), continue to teach me what true poetry is.

About the Author

DANTE DI STEFANO is the author of four poetry collections and a chapbook, including, the book-length poem, *Midwhistle* (University of Wisconsin Press, 2023). His writing has appeared in the Academy of American Poets *Poem-a-Day*, *American Poetry Review*, *Best American Poetry 2018*, *Prairie Schooner*, *The Sewanee Review*, *The Writer's Chronicle*, and elsewhere. He holds a PhD in English Literature from Binghamton University. His poetry has won numerous awards, including the Auburn Witness Poetry Prize, the Manchester Poetry Prize (UK), the Red Hen Press Poetry Award, the Thayer Fellowship in the Arts, among others. He co-edited the anthology *Misrepresented People* (NYQ Books, 2018) and lives in Endwell, NY with his wife and two children.

VIA Folios

A refereed book series dedicated to the culture of Italians and Italian Americans.

FRED GARDAPHÈ. *Moustache Pete is Dead! Long Live Moustache Pete!*.
  Vol 13. Oral Literature.

JONE GAILLARD CORSI. *Il libretto d'autore. 1860 - 1930*. Vol 12. Criticism.

HELEN BAROLINI. *Chiaroscuro: Essays of Identity*. Vol 11. Essays.

PICARAZZI & FEINSTEIN, Eds. *An African Harlequin in Milan*.
  Vol 10. Theater/Essays.

JOSEPH RICAPITO. *Florentine Streets & Other Poems*. Vol 9. Poetry.

FRED MISURELLA. *Short Time*. Vol 8. Novella.

NED CONDINI. *Quartettsatz*. Vol 7. Poetry.

ANTHONY JULIAN TAMBURRI, Ed. *Fuori: Essays by Italian/American
  Lesbiansand Gays*. Vol 6. Essays.

ANTONIO GRAMSCI. P. Verdicchio. Trans. & Intro. *The Southern Question*.
  Vol 5. Social Criticism.

DANIELA GIOSEFFI. *Word Wounds & Water Flowers*. Vol 4. Poetry. $8

WILEY FEINSTEIN. *Humility's Deceit: Calvino Reading Ariosto Reading Calvino*.
  Vol 3. Criticism.

PAOLO A. GIORDANO, Ed. *Joseph Tusiani: Poet. Translator. Humanist*.
  Vol 2. Criticism.

ROBERT VISCUSI. *Oration Upon the Most Recent Death of Christopher Columbus*.
  Vol 1. Poetry.